MARIN SORESCU

SELECTED POEMS

Also by Marin Sorescu

POETRY

Let's Talk about the Weather (Forest Books, 1985)
The Biggest Egg in the World (Bloodaxe Books, 1987)

PLAYS

The Thirst of the Salt Mountain (Forest Books, 1985)
 [trilogy of *Jonah*, *The Verger* and *The Matrix*]
Vlad Dracula the Impaler (Forest Books, 1987)

Marin Sorescu
Selected Poems

TRANSLATED BY MICHAEL HAMBURGER

BLOODAXE BOOKS

ISBN: 0 906427 48 7

First published 1983 by
Bloodaxe Books Ltd,
P.O. Box 1SN,
Newcastle upon Tyne NE99 1SN.

Second impression 1993.

Bloodaxe Books Ltd acknowledges
the financial assistance of Northern Arts.

Typesetting by
Tyneside Free Press Workshop Ltd, Newcastle upon Tyne.

Cover printing by J. Thomson Colour Printers Ltd, Glasgow.

Printed in Great Britain by
Cromwell Press Ltd, Broughton Gifford, Melksham, Wiltshire.

Acknowledgements

Acknowledgements are due to the editors of *Poetry* (Chicago) and *Stand*, where some of these translations first appeared. Some of the translations appear in a small selection of Marin Sorescu's poems published in 1982 by Logbridge-Rhodes (Durango, Colorado).

Contents

SOUL, YOU ARE GOOD FOR ANYTHING/
SUFLETE, BUN LA TOATE (1972)

SO/*ASTFEL* (1973)

Introduction

Marin Sorescu was born in 1936 in Oltenia, Romania, and began to publish while studying philosophy at the University of Iassy. After graduating he did editorial work for a newspaper, and he has continued to be closely associated with a succession of periodicals, both as a contributor and as an editor. At present he edits the magazine *Ramuri*.

After an early book of verse parodies, his first major collection of poems appeared in 1965, followed by many others and by paperback selections from all his books of poems. He is also a playwright—his play *Jonah* has been performed in several European countries—an essayist, translator, and writer of children's books. In 1969 he won the gold medal awarded at the International Poetry Festival in Naples, and he has received major awards for his plays and poems in Romania. In 1971 he read at the Edinburgh Festival; and at the International Poetry Festival in Berlin in 1978, in Morelia, Mexico in 1981, and in Madrid in 1982. In 1971-72 he was a member of the International Writing Program at the University of Iowa. In 1973-74 he was a visiting writer in West Berlin.

Translations of Sorescu's poems and plays have appeared in many countries. A selection of poems, *Frames*, translated into English by Roy McGregor-Hastie, was published in Bucharest and Iowa City in 1972. An English version of one of Sorescu's plays, *The Impaler's Third Stake*, appeared in the English-language *Romanian Review*, 9-10 (1980). Two volumes of selected poems in Oskar Pastior's German versions appeared in West Germany in 1974 and 1975, and a third book of poems translated by Pastior is about to be published; an East German selection of translations by various hands was published in 1976.

I mention these German translations because I am indebted to them for my versions. My understanding of Romanian is confined to the recognition of Latin roots, where there are such roots, and that means it amounts to very little, though I can get a sense of the shape and movement of a poem on the page. I have worked in part from literal English versions given to me by Sorescu; but Oskar Pastior's German versions had the irresistible distinction of being by a poet born in Romania who writes in German, with outstanding virtuosity and brilliance.

Like many East European poets who began to write after the war, Sorescu felt it necessary to make a clean break with the Romantic-Symbolist assumptions that had dominated Western poetry up to that time, when French culture exercised a powerful influence in Romania. The officially prescribed alternative, "socialist realism", proved of little use to lyrical poets. Those whose "social consciousness" was ideologically directed tended less towards anything that could be called "realism" than to various modes of didacticism, exhortation or "agit-prop". Those with more independence of mind tended towards a "minimal poetry", often elliptic, laconic, depersonalized, or masked under an assumed impersonality.

Sorescu's alternative was a freedom of invention that could strike superficial readers as "surrealist". Yet Sorescu's procedures are as far removed as possible from surrealism, despite the dream-like situations set up in many of his poems. Surrealism demanded a liberation of the subconscious and aspired to automatic writing. Sorescu's verse parables approach human realities by way of fantasy and irony; not, however, to liberate the subconscious, his own or anyone else's, but rather to arrive at truths that have to do with human existence on a conscious level. It is the interplay of fantasy and irony that sets his work as far apart from surrealism as from a mimetic, photographic realism.

What he shares with other post-war East European poets is a vocabulary deliberately flat, everyday, commonplace; but in the context of his parables this seemingly casual, even random "low mimetic" vocabulary becomes deeply subversive of the attitudes of mind on which it usually rests. Like his compatriot Ionesco, Sorescu is a specialist in the absurd.

Although I have read a good deal of contemporary Romanian poetry in translation, I cannot presume to "place" Sorescu's work within a national tradition. Yet his pervasive, generous irony above all—generous, because it does not spare his own seriousness, his own aspirations, his own sensibility any more than it spares other people's—strikes me as a national characteristic. This irony can be seen as deeply and truly egalitarian in spirit. Unlike the irony of Corbière and Laforgue that was carried over into American poetry by Ezra Pound and T.S. Eliot, Sorescu's does not serve to distance his poetic person from the general run of humanity, or to spice a self-consciousness that could otherwise lapse into confessional mawkishness. Sorescu's parables ironize the human condition, including his own; and they do so impartially, with a minimum of bias towards any one social order, group or class. This makes for universality—and for translatability. Yet national, even regional, preoccupations can be compatible with both.

One such preoccupation is Sorescu's with the Roman past, as in the poem 'To the Sea', his tribute to Ovid, who was exiled to Tomi on the Black (or Euxine) Sea, and died there. Another is with the rites of the Orthodox Church—still the official Church of Romania, under Communism. Sorescu's irony extends even to his religious allusions, but so does the seriousness that underlies his irony everywhere.

Sorescu has commented on the close connections, for him, between the writing of plays and the writing of poems; and some of his poems also come close to being stories of a kind. Very few of them are strictly lyrical, if only because Sorescu is deeply suspicious of the emotive effects at which strictly lyrical verse excels. For related reasons his poems avoid the tensions and the density that come of a poet's close engagement with particulars, the quiddity of one thing, one place, one person, rather than a situation that could be anyone's. For that Sorescu would have had to resort to a more specialized, more individual vocabulary, a verbal texture less transparent than his own. Every kind of poetry takes its own kind of risks, and Sorescu has taken the very great risks involved in trying to wrench poetry out of its specialization. At his best he has brought that off, thanks to his all-embracing irony, comic inventiveness, and sheer intelligence.

MICHAEL HAMBURGER

from *Poeme* (1965)

In the Morning

Sun, with your lather we wash,
our essential soap
put out for us
on the shelf of the sky.
Towards you we extend our arms
and with light we rub ourselves over
till with so much pleasure our bones begin to ache.

Oh, the delight
of mornings on this earth!
As in a boarding school washroom
when children fill their mouths with water
and drench one another.

We don't yet know where to find
the very best towels –
so still it's with death
that we dry our faces.

'With a green scarf'

With a green scarf I blindfolded
the eyes of the trees
and asked them to catch me.

At once the trees caught me,
their leaves shaking with laughter.

I blindfolded the birds
with a scarf of clouds
and asked them to catch me.

The birds caught me
with a song.

Then with a smile I blindfolded
my sorrow
and the day after it caught me
with a love.

I blindfolded the sun
with my nights
and asked the sun to catch me.

I know where you are, the sun said,
just behind that time.
Don't bother to hide any longer.

Don't bother to hide any longer,
said all of them,
as well as all the feelings
I tried to blindfold.

The Way

Thoughtful, hands behind my back,
I walk between the rails
the straightest way
there is.

From behind me
at great speed
comes a train
that knows nothing of me.

This train
(old Zeno is my witness)
will never reach me
for I am always a little ahead
of things that don't think.

And even if brutally
it runs me over
there will always be someone
to walk ahead of it,
his head full of things,
hands behind his back.

Someone like me,
now,
while the black monster
approaches horribly fast
and will never
catch up with me.

Leda

Smiling, Leda mixes
in with things
and sleeps with
everyone.

To the fence in the yard she gives
an ivy baby,
to the sun thing up there
a sunflower.

Shamelessly she did it
with all the oxen,
beginning with Apis,
but, damn it, to look at her
no one would have guessed.

A fine little piece,
that Leda.
Which is why the world
still remains so lovely.

The Sacred Flame

Throw a few more logs
on to the sun,
in a few billion years,
they say, it will
go out.

When there's no firewood left
you can use the meadows
that could just as well have been woodland,
then the mountains, the moon and the sky
of which we don't know for sure
that they are not wood.

Just keep throwing
something on to it,
a few logs,
a few lives.

For look, already a flicker
passes over our faces,
now they are handsome, now ugly,
now they are day, now they're night,
now they are seasons, now years.

Flight

One day
I shall rise from my desk
and slowly walk away from my words,
from you
and from all things.

I shall see a mountain on the horizon
and walk towards it
until the mountain is left behind.

Then I shall follow a cloud
and the cloud will be left behind.

And the sun will be left behind
and the stars
and the whole universe . . .

Chess

I move a white day,
he moves a black day.
I rush forward with a dream,
he takes it from me in war.
He attacks my lungs,
for a year I lie thinking in hospital,
calculate brilliantly
and win a black day.
He displaces a misfortune
and threatens me with cancer
(which at the moment moves diagonally)
but I treat him to a book
and force him to retreat,
take a few other pieces and
notice that half my life has
vanished from the board.
'I shall call checkmate
and you will lose your optimism,'
he claims.
'Never mind,' I try to joke,
'then I'll switch to feelings and castle your king.'

Behind me my wife, my children,
the sun, the moon and other spectators
tremble at every move I make.

I light a cigarette
and continue the game.

Wheel

I live inside a wheel,
a fact brought home to me
by the trees;
whenever I look through the window
their leaves
now are up,
now are down.

By the birds too.
They fly
south with one wing,
north with the other.

And by the sun,
as it rises
in my left eye today,
in my right eye tomorrow,

and by myself,
here today,
gone tomorrow.

Illness

Doctor, I feel a fatal something
here, in the area of my being.
Every organ hurts,
by day the sun is in pain,
at night it's the moon and the stars.

I feel a stitch in that cloud in the sky
which I'd never noticed before,
and every morning I wake up
with a sensation of winter.

In vain I've taken all sorts of drugs:
I've hated and loved, I've learnt to read
and I've even read a number of books.
I've talked to people and I've done some thinking,
I've been kind and I've been handsome.
But none of it, doctor, has done any good,
for all the years I have spent.

That day I was born,
I've every reason to fear,
I must have caught my death.

Portrait of the Artist

I left my shoes
to the road.
As for my trousers, I slipped them over
the trees, right up to the leaves.
My jacket I wrapped
round the wind's shoulders.
I put my old hat
on the first cloud
that came my way.

Then I stepped back
into death
to observe myself.

My self-portrait
was a faithful one.

The resemblance was so close
that quite spontaneously people –
I had forgotten to sign it –
inscribed my name
on a stone.

Shakespeare

Shakespeare created the world in seven days.

On the first day he made the sky and the mountains and
                              the ravines of the soul.
On the second day he made the rivers, the seas, the oceans
                              as well as
the other feelings and
gave them to Hamlet, to Julius Caesar, to Cleopatra, Ophelia,
Othello and others, to
reign over them with their children and later descendants
for ever and ever.

On the third day he summoned the whole of humanity
to teach them the diverse tastes:
the taste of happiness, that of love, the taste
of despair, of jealousy, fame etc.,
till there were none left to distribute. But then
a few people came who were late.
Sorry for them, the creator patted their heads and informed
                              them
there was nothing left for them save
to become literary critics and
debunk his work.

The fourth and fifth days he reserved for laughter, gave
the clowns a free hand, allowed them
to turn somersaults and so provided amusement for
kings and emperors and other unfortunate persons.
On the sixth day he dealt with administrative problems:
he set up a storm
and taught King Lear
how to wear a crown of straw.

There was some waste matter, too, from creation, and out
                              of this
he made Richard III.
On the seventh day he made sure that nothing was left undone.
Already theatre managers had plastered
the whole world with their playbills, and

Shakespeare thought that after so much hard work
he deserved to see a performance;
but meanwhile, because he felt so excessively drowsy,
he lay down to take
forty winks of death.

Impulse

Evening after evening
I collect all the available chairs
in the neighbourhood
and read them poems.

Chairs are most receptive
to poetry,
if the seating order is right.

In the process
I become excited
and tell them
for hours
how beautifully my soul
communed
that day.

Usually our meetings
are matter-of-fact,
free of sentimental
wallowing.

In any case
you can say
that each of us
has done his duty,
and we can make
a new start.

The Sea Shell

I have hidden inside a sea shell
but forgotten in which.

Now daily I dive,
filtering the sea through my fingers,
to find myself.
Sometimes I think
a giant fish has swallowed me.
Looking for it everywhere I want to make sure
it will get me completely.

The sea-bed attracts me, and
I'm repelled by millions
of sea shells that all look alike.
Help, I am one of them.
If only I knew, which.

How often I've gone straight up
to one of them, saying: That's me.
Only, when I prised it open
it was empty.

Late

It's grown late
inside me.
Look, it's turning dark
in my right hand,
in the acacia in front of the house.

With one eyelid's flicker
I must
put out all things
that are shining still,
the slippers beside my bed,
the clothes rack, the pictures . . .
As for my other goods and chattels –
all I can see around me
up to the stars above –
there's no point in taking them with me,
let them go on shining.

And in my will I've requested
that to honour
my memory,
at least on the more solemn days of remembrance,
the whole universe shall be distributed
among the people, as alms.

from *Moartea Ceasului* (1966)

Prayer

O saints,
let me join your company
if only as an extra.

You are old,
perhaps your years are beginning to hurt you,
those years that in layers of paint
have retouched your being.

Let me carry out
the less important work
in the niches, the nooks.

At the Last Supper, for instance
I could
eat light
and blow out your haloes
when the service is over.

And from time to time,
half a walk away,
I could make my hands a trumpet
and, once for the believers,
once for the unbelievers, could shout
Hallelujah! Hallelujah!

Poisons

Grass, mountains, waters, the sky
have mixed with my blood
and now I am waiting
for the effect.

I feel myself turning green
because of the grass,

feel chasms form inside me
and fog,
because of the mountains.

Feel how the stones on the road are turned
to pebbles by my feet
and keep looking out for the sea
because of the waters.

And inside me I also feel
a kind of blueness, boundlessness,
with stars on my eyes
and on my fingertips.

Superstition

My cat washes
with her left paw,
there will be another war.

For I have observed
that whenever she washes
with her left paw
international tension grows
considerably.

How can she possibly keep her eye
on all the five continents?
Could it be
that in her pupils
that Pythia now resides
who has the power
to predict
the whole of history
without a full-stop or comma?

It's enough to make me howl
when I think that I
and the Heaven with its souls I have
shouldered
in the last resort
depend
on the whims of a cat.

Go and catch mice,
don't unleash
more world wars,
damned
lazybones!

Abyss

God is deaf.
So if I have something to say to him
I resort to paper.
That's what one does with anyone
who's deaf.

But he can't make out my handwriting;
and when I see how, confronted
with a conjunction, he scratches himself
behind his aureole, I reflect how much simpler it would be
to yell it all into his ears.

That's what I do.
But the good Lord shakes his head,
he can't hear me,
and he makes signs that everything
I wish to convey to him
is to be written down.

I succumb to despair,
I go out into the street
and stop passers-by,
show them my so neatly and legibly written
scripts, penned for God's eye,
while the people, by no means deaf
but merely in a hurry,
push the paper away
and ask me to tell them briefly,
succinctly, what it's about.

Then I roar
as though from an abyss,
roar as God roars
when he says his prayers.

And in terror that I myself could already be deaf
I blurt out the things
I had meant to say to them.

Omens

If you meet a chair,
that is good, you will go to Heaven.
If you meet a mountain,
that is bad, you'll go to the chair.
If you meet the Great Bear,
that is good, you will go to Heaven.
If you meet a snail.
that is bad, you'll go to the snail.
If you meet a woman,
that is good, you will go to Heaven.
If you meet a tablecloth,
that is bad, you'll go to the cupboard.
If you meet a snake,
that is good, it will die and you'll go to Heaven.
If the snake meets you,
that is bad, you will die and the snake go to Heaven.

If you die,
that's bad, bad.

Beware of this omen
and of all others.

from *Tineretea lui Don Quijote* (1968)

Toys

We horribly grown-up people
who on the ice between the two wars
never once fell down
or, if we did ever slip,
at once broke a year, one
of our distinguished stucco-stiff
plaster years . . .
oh, we horribly grown-up people
grow aware at times how
much we lack toys
to play with.

We have all we need,
only no toys.
Our longing is for the optimism
in the cotton wool hearts of dolls
and for our ship, the
three-master that sails the seas
and
the land.

We should love to mount a wooden horse,
it would neigh, from deep down its wood, and we
should say: 'Move off with us,
take us no matter where,
for everywhere in life
we have great things to do.'

Oh, how badly sometimes we need such a toy!
But we can't even be sad
about it, grip
the leg of a chair and
weep from deep down in our souls,
for we're very big, very grown-up, and
there's no one bigger, more grown-up than we are
to comfort us.

Essay

Life begins with the reptiles:
the amoeba, the snails, the spiders,
the water with a tusk on each wave,
the space-hungry paths,
the roots, when they're hungry.

Even the minerals
devour one another.
A diamond has all the others
inside its guts.

What we see as vertical
is the various forms
of courtship dances which,
in poplars for instance, come close to being sublime,
in mountain ranges, to being grotesque,
in snakes, to being rainbows.
At night from the moon rattles
the hour of multiplication,
even seeds are on heat;
wax grows most frenzied of all.

The fishes, the birds, the mammals with great hopes
(among them humans too)
lay their eggs straight into sand
which they forget as soon as the kiss is over.

As you can see,
everything round about is perfect
as a sphere
containing neither an angle
nor a broken line
with which one could hang oneself.

Perspective

If you moved away a little
my love would grow
like the air between us.

If you moved away quite far
I should love you with the mountains,
waters and cities
that lie between us.

If you moved away once more
by one horizon
your profile would comprise
the sun, the moon and half the sky.

Perpetuum Mobile

Between people's
ideals
and their realization
there is always
a greater drop
than in the highest
of waterfalls.

This potential gradient
can be exploited
rationally,
if we build a sort of
power station above it.

The energy it supplies,
even if we use it only
to light our cigarettes,
is something
anyway;
for while one is smoking
one can very seriously
think up
ideals even crazier.

This Hour

This hour
when all things, tired of meaning,
fall asleep over it,
like guards
with their chins resting
on their lances.

Walls, rafters, skies and universe,
please don't rest too heavily
on me,
I too rest on a thought,
indeed on a single word
that already
at one of its ends
is beginning
to cease to be.

Start

Often the start went wrong,
the bang wasn't loud enough
or it wasn't heard,
and the competitors, sent back again and again to their places,
became so nervous that they began to brawl,
covered themselves in ashes, broke
their legs and threw sand into
the spectators' eyes.

The track, the whole stadium,
was often red with blood,
the start went wrong so many times.

Once
a man with the starting-gun
out of fear of the imminent disaster
fired not into the air
but through his head.
As though by a miracle this time
all the runners won.
The death of the shot man
was hardly noticed.

Ever since, tradition demands,
whoever signals the start
puts the weapon to his forehead.

The instrument that brought in so many gold medals
has landed up with me.

Already the runners rest
their left knees on the chalk line,
their eyes have run on far ahead,
their nostrils quiver.

All they're waiting for is the bang.
It's all up to me.

Movement

First thing in the morning –
words to be bridled,
saddled.
The grass, complete with bridle
and saddle,
every pore bridled,
an infinite stud,
stamping infinity.

Stamping, the stones, with impatience.
The hour stamping,
in each sentence the yeast for
happiness
again and again.

All things are bridled,
all saddled.

Who is to ride them, my God,
when I too
am bridled and saddled?
And you, are you not
bridled and saddled?

The Complaint

They have murdered my time,
Your Honour.

When of my own free will
I returned from the war
I realized
that my time,
heart, mouth and forehead
had been amputated.

But they still wouldn't leave it alone,
it had to absolve days of torment,
days of tears, days of machines, days of oxen
and many other things
it did not care for.

After that they began
to use it for testing
a number of poisons,
griefs and cares –
that's what they called them.

They finished me off
with a well-aimed
blow of fate.

With all due respect,
that wasn't a life.
Meanwhile, in order
to voice my complaint,
I have wasted half my death
standing in queues
here,
at the Last Judgement.

Reading Matter

As usual
this day is pushed into my room
from under the door.

I put on my spectacles
and begin to
read it.

Nothing of any importance,
as far as I can see.
Towards noon, a slight depression
with no reasons given,
and, it says,
I shall take up
my trend towards light
at the point where I broke off yesterday.

The foreign branch
gives information about my transactions
with water, with mountains and with the air,
about their absurd demand
to enter my bloodstream and
my brain.

Then the usual reports
about working conditions,
the way to the bread bin,
the cheerful mood
(but not a word
about conditions
in the liver region).

Where on earth do they print
this stuff,
my life,
when it's full of
inadmissible
errors.

from *Tusiti* (1970)

The Crate

I was by the sea
and distributed boats,
vague ones, things
built more for the contemplation of water, who knows
whether seaworthy, navigable at all, perhaps they were
                                        telescopes,
yet one had to board them and voyage
in them on water, to see the world.

Then two strangers came along
and asked for a boat, for they too wanted to voyage.
Only, there wasn't one left,
much as I searched—in vain,
they'd run out on me early that day,
there were never enough of them for the crowds, the crowds
                                        on the coast.
I examined the two: serious people,
so I found a crate for them that was lying around,
and a bit of rag, a bit of string, take them and go,
for they really wanted to voyage, as one could see.

And I felt sorry for them,
and they boarded the crate,
the sea is close here, not two steps away, as all could see,
but where does it end!
And those two in the crate.

The sea does not truly belong
to the territory of Earth;
it alone, now and again de-
taching itself, draws cloud after cloud over the sky.
That, presumably, is what they wished to find out.
Hence their haste.

I'm convinced they relied
on the drops of water even that would evaporate as they
passed over them; they themselves were about to get away
and had forces in them that lifted them up,
so that both managed a hovering

and the crate, which had by no means been caulked,
did not sink with them . . .

For a long time they had been land-
lubbers, as it were, had ascertained
that they did not evaporate, and asked
themselves why it was that the earth too,
so as to be lighter, didn't evaporate now and
again, mount the clouds and
come down as rain in boulders
as large as the olive branch
which the Flood made the dove
drop from its beak.

That is why they simply had to go out to sea
and came and found me lolling about on the sand,
dreaming of sailing-boats, or rather, having just finished
                                                dreaming
and having distributed all of them early that day,
with only this imperfect crate left over,
into which they hurled themselves, rashly, for they were young,
and now I see them hover away above me,
more and more distant, smaller and smaller,
and, saving up new sleep, I wear myself out for others.

Symmetry

As I was walking along
suddenly two paths
opened up for me:
one to the left,
the other to the right,
and quite symmmetrical.

I stopped,
blinked,
bit either lip in turn,
cleared my throat and
took the one to the right
(just the wrong one,
it turned out later).

So now I followed it.
Never mind the details.
And then suddenly
two chasms
opened up for me:
one to the left,
the other to the right.
Without thinking I dropped
headlong
into the one to the left, which, alas,
just wasn't the one padded with down!
On all fours I crawled on,
and as I crawled
suddenly
two open paths lay before me.
Just wait, I said to myself,
and this time took the one to the left.
Straight into misery.
The wrong choice, quite wrong; to the right
led the True, the Only, the Great one, *the*
Way, so it seemed.
Well, at the next fork
I put my trust,
body and soul, into the one on the right. Once more

it was the other which . . .
Now my pack is almost empty,
my gnarled stick, grown old,
no longer puts out leaves
that could give me shade
when despair takes hold of me.
My legs are worn down,
the stumps grumble and growl
that, no matter where I went,
it was one great mistake.

And suddenly now
two Heavens
open up for me:
one to the right,
the other to the left.

The Halberd

An overcrowded bus,
a madhouse.
People embrace parcels,
microbes, viruses.
From my seat
behind me I notice
an old man with a spade,
the devil knows why he's lugging it home,
he holds it planted upright
on its shaft like a halberd
before the Emperor's time.

The old man is old as the world,
he has a patch over his right eye
and a trembling hand.
Any moment, curse it, he'll let go of the spade,
it will drop on my head, I think.

In other ways he seems friendly enough,
courteous,
almost talkative.
Don't worry, he says, I'm holding on bloody tight
to the bloody spade –
and yet from time to time it falls,
clank clank clank!
Three-quarters of the passengers already have bruises on their
heads.
Again and again the old man lets go of the spade,
again and again he curses it and apologizes.
I can't help it, sorry,
but there's no cause for alarm,
don't panic, please,
I assure you, this bloody spade
won't fall again now or ever again in the future,
as you see, I'm holding it tight.
And no sooner said than—clank!

Well, the road just isn't smooth,
bumps are bumps.
Yes, and the driver up in front doesn't seem to notice.
Does his shift, why should he care,
his job to convey passengers, living or dead, it's all the same.
If that weren't so, why doesn't he halt at the stops,
why doesn't he halt anywhere,
when this half-witted criminal could simply be dumped,
all the more because, as I see,
he has finished off nearly all the passengers
and is about to
take up position behind me with his halberd.

Listen to me, driver!
But who can hear me now,
the bus rushes on, perhaps it's running late,
the bumps get worse,
the old man has begun to talk to me,
he's getting more and more courteous
and we start to talk about the weather.

The Actors

How strangely limber these actors are!
How good they are
at living for us with their shirtsleeves rolled up!

Never have I seen a more perfect kiss
than theirs in the third act
when their feelings
are being made clear.

Spotty, smeared with oil,
with caps true to life,
performing all sorts of functions,
they come and go as they're prompted
by words that roll out like red carpets.

Their deaths on the boards are so natural
that the real, the
once and for all tragically
made-up dead of the graveyards
seem to stir
at such perfection.

And how much more we, who woodenly
are stuck in a single life!
And are not competent to live that one even.
We who talk nonsense or keep silent for centuries,
awkward and unaesthetic,
not knowing what to do with our hands.

History Therapy

When at night in bed
I can't get to sleep
I take an historical atlas
with a mouthful of water.

While I wait for it to work
I trace with my finger
the Hittite Kingdom
but soon have to start
again from scratch,

for really the Hittite Kingdom
is the Egyptian Kingdom,
no, the Assyrian . . .
the Median and Chaldean . . .
the Persian . . .

If that is so, I reflect,
I may as well
go
to sleep.

Besides Me

In this woman's bathroom
somebody hides.

She talks with me,
she loves me truly,
but always somebody stirs in her soul,
who's there, besides me.
I read in her eyes,
in her hair,
in her line of life
that this house has only one entrance
and that she conceals from me
somebody in her bathroom.

Or, it could be, in the neighbour's house,
or in another house
anywhere in the street,
in another town, or in the woods,
or on the sea bed.

Somebody hides
who spies on my thoughts,
who listens in on my deathless feelings,
who looks at his watch.

'If the water doesn't turn black'

If the water doesn't turn black
one's pleasure in washing
is reduced to nothing,
said Pontius Pilate, freely soaping his hands.

Meanwhile Jesus is mocked,
crucified,
forced to squirm on the cross
as though it were bed.

They let him swallow poison,
they let him die,
they let him rise on the third day,
they let him ascend to Heaven.

Meanwhile the cross is burnt,
firewood chopped from crusades,
through the chinks between nations
corrosive smoke curls up,
gunpowder begins,
radiation fallout proclaims the rise of the new age.

Finally
the waste water grows dirtier and dirtier,
history takes its course,
and with increasing pleasure
Pontius Pilate
washes
and rubs
his hands.

View

How generous nature
has been to us!
We could easily
have propagated our kind with spores
(as one often finds with things like plants!) –

gusts of wind
and at once
spores rise from our hair
like swarms into nothing,
a kiss into blue air,
words into the wind,
a streak
of mist.

Then there'd be children
and children and
we'd be left with nothing and should
have grasped nothing at all of this life,
that the two of us are a couple, the last,
each with a view.

Tobacco

To the dead
eternity seems
longer
because they're forbidden
to smoke.

We living people puff,
take a light from
one another and
emit our thanks
through our noses.

A cigarette when you're born,
another when you go to school,
yet another for your wedding;
a cigarette because it's raining,
and because it isn't raining,
another . . .

You don't even notice
how in no time like this
with cheap tobacco
you've blown
your life's work away.

Friends

Come on, let's kill ourselves, I say to my friends.
Today we communicated so well,
we were all so sad,
never again shall we rise to
that point of perfection together;
to hesitate now would be a sin.

In the bath, I believe, it's most tragic,
so let's do it the way the enlightened Romans did it,
opening their veins
while discoursing on the nature of love.
Friends, the water's been heated,
let's begin, I will count: one, two, three . . .

Not without astonishment I noted in Hell
that I was on my own.
For some it's harder, I told myself,
some have all sorts of ties;
it can't be that they were making a fool of me: a man's word
                                                  counts for something,
but the passage of time . . .

True enough, Hell wasn't a bed of roses for me,
especially at first, with nobody about
I could really talk to,
but gradually I found company, made friends.

A circle quite extraordinarily close-knit.
We discussed a number of theories,
felt in excellent spirits
and even got as far as suicide.

. . . And again I found myself alone, in Purgatory.
Looking around, for a kindred soul or two,
and yet, although the occupants of Purgatory,
in their inter-territorial uncertainty,
are very prone to suspicion –
a girl is fond of me, she loves me, she's good-looking,
we have moments of great ecstasy. It's incredible, marvellous!

I'm about to propose . . .
Knowing better now, I leave it to her,
before taking the plunge.
The girl does what she does, and is alive again –
and I'm alone in Heaven.
Never has anyone got this far,
I am the first, the world exists as a project;
a very vague affair
in the mind of God,
with whom meanwhile I have made friends.

On all levels, it seems, there is sadness.
God is in despair,
I gaze into his empty eyes and lose myself.
He whirls into the chasms of my deaths.
We understand each other splendidly,
my God, I believe it couldn't be better.
It's your turn. Or what do you say
to leaving it all in the dark?

Carbon Paper

Someone overnight sticks a gigantic
sheet of carbon paper on my door.
Everything I am thinking immediately
comes through on the other side of the wall.

Inquisitive people from all over the place
come in throngs, I hear the soles of their shoes
lift up the stairs to my apartment
and, leaving,
put them down again.

They are birds of every species,
moon farm dogs,
transitions, forest aisles and
old acacias that
suffer from insomnia.

They put on spectacles and
read me, are moved or
threaten me with their fists, it
depends, for I have a
clear idea of it all.

Only about my soul
I know nothing.
About my soul that perpetually
slides away from me between days,
like a cake of soap
in the bath.

The Investigation

Everything crawls with evidence
that no one examines.
Here you have leaf veins
that must lead to something.
After all, each of them
could put us on the track.

So now we form two detachments equal in strength
and proceed separately,
I and the dog Osman,
the old one; yet his nose for the scent is fresh as dew.
The crimes he's detected already!
Look out!

You can see, already he's on the
trail of a suspect ant:
Where does it drag the grains,
what, you didn't enquire?
Osman, who's watching its ways,
has nodded off on the job.
He's not going to keep his eyes
open till darkness falls
like any lookout man,
not at his age.

Amongst other things I must catch a butterfly
and arrest a dream
that passed through my eye-
flaps last night and now
hides God knows where.

There's much to be uncovered and brought to light.
But around noon the investigation is suspended
because both I and the other equal detachment
—the dog Osman, the old one—
have agreed unanimously
that nothing so stimulates one's appetite
as a world full of villainies.

The Organ Danger

Organs are a danger, and for this
reason (anyway, one has first-hand experience
of the things)—that they have too many pipes, that
is, too many pipes at the *same time*
and one never knows what's concealed inside them
(it could be nothing, even that is
a possibility) but
how uncannily threatening over there
in the cathedral's depth they loom
up to Heaven, in a cloud of incense,
at any moment the firing mechanism
could go off—and, in my opinion at least,
this is not the moment at all
to despatch all music fans up to Heaven.

Who knows what flames, in rank and file,
hiss through the many connected vents.
It's enough to put the wind up anyone.

Their throats should be packed with sawdust
so that they cease to be out of tune for no
understandable reason, the longer pipes should be
clipped a bit, and altogether they should be
welded apart and provided with such spaces
that they no longer look so much like mass-
organs. . . Or they could be left
in principle
experimentally
as they are,
only tipped over on to
the floor, as a sort of sensitive catwalk
on which the orchestra could play.

I have debated these matters with
the organists. They would not budge
from their position.

from *Suflete, bun la toate* (1972)

Seneca

When the sun goes down, they told me,
I have to slash my veins;
it's only noon,
I've a few hours left to live.

Shall I write to Lucullus?
I don't feel like it now.
Go to the circus?
I don't need games any more, nor bread.
Shall I tell
philosophy's fortune?

Another hour has gone by.
I've a full four hours left.
My bath water's heating up.
I yawn and lean out of the window,
follow the course of the sun that will not go down again,
and feel inexpressibly bored.

Precautions

I put on my armour,
stones the storm left behind.

Through spectacles
at the back of my neck
I see only
what in retrospect
was the right thing.

Arms, legs, thoughts –
I wrap them all in plastic,
not one inch remains for caresses
or contact with
other poisons.

Even the heart inside me
I've put away
inside the plating of
a tortoise 800 years old.

It's time now,
gently I answer her:
and I like you too.

The Glass Wall

To make the one world in which we live
more comfortable,
with a glass wall we have divided it
into two zones.

Every advance, of course,
has its drawbacks.
If, for instance, one feels
like having a good bath,
one now has to cross over
into the other world
to get the soap.

All the same,
each one of us can boast
of a two-world apartment
(furnished in different styles,
it goes without saying)
with a communal sun, for the moment,
and separate access
to earth.

Dictation

The past photographs the present.
Hold it there,
make a war,
not this one, the other,
though you've killed vastly in vain,
doesn't matter,
smile,
that's right, look at love,
look at Monday,
look at Tuesday, at Wednesday,
discover something,
a principle, a continent, a conspiracy,
anything,
move mountains,
shrug your shoulders –
that's it,
thanks.

The Thieves

One of my poems kept me awake at night,
so I sent it into the country
to a grandfather.

After that I wrote another
and sent it to my mother
to store in her attic.

I still wrote several more
and with misgivings entrusted them to relations
who promised to keep them with care.

And so forth; for every new poem
there was someone to take it in.
Since each of my friends
in his turn has
a friend he keeps quiet about.

And now even I don't remember
where this and that line might be,
and if I were to fall among thieves
and they tortured me too, the most I could tell them
is that those dubious things
are somewhere in the country
and safe.

Question

What's today?
A Monday?
But Monday was
last week.

Tuesday?
But it was Tuesday all last year,
nothing but Tuesday.

Wednesday?
The century before this one, as far as I know,
fell on a Wednesday.

Thursday?
On a Thursday
Carthage was sacked,
on a Thursday
the Library in Alexandria burned.
Don't tell me that since then
not one day has passed.

Friday? Saturday?
Yes I've heard
of those days.
No fairy tales, please.

Sunday perhaps?
The time before the Creation
was called Sunday.
I remember that.

You see, all the days of the week *have been*.
For us there's no new one
left.

Soul, You Are Good for Anything

Soul, you are good for anything!
For looking out of the window
into the dark,
for looking at women go by,
for judging the distance
between two gnats.

Perhaps we misuse you
as a brush,
as a sponge,
as a star,
as a telescope,
as a cloth.

You tunnel the soul like moles
in the light of an air that dazzles:
What claws does one need to travel through light,
and how drive adits there?

I think you disturb us,
you're too far ahead of us, soul,
soul, you are good for anything.

Attempt to Escape

Perhaps one could see
stars in the daytime too
if they weren't concealed by
butterflies that
all night long
circle the earth
on their wings.

There is a gravity, too,
that pulls a thing skywards,
with a powerful pumping system
its light sucks in
the butterflies.

The air itself is a fluttering
rise of a wing
up to the giant burning-glass.

I look up.
If there's a star
above me
without fail I move away
as far as I can
from the place.

But there are so many stars
that above us
always
one star hangs.

from *Astfel* (1973)

Closeness

How small this country is!
The long black eyelashes of
the women, so that they don't
stick out beyond the frontier,
are fastened with clasps at the back of their necks –
those eyelashes grown too long.

From time to time, too,
the dead are shifted,
to be pounded down with steam hammers
and mixed into concrete,
for the country is very small.

Only now and then
the graves are forced open
and pipes laid in;
the cold drinking water
flows through my
grandfather's skull.

How cold this water is
that carries twiglets of fir
although the mountains are far away;
but my grandfather rambled there
and keeps it all in mind.

Perpetuum Mobile

At least Prometheus still had the right to object.
But what if, fixed to the rock there,
unable to stir and inwardly minced,
what he managed to say was only:
'Why the liver, of all things?'

Yes indeed, the simplest
and seemingly tritest objection:
'Why the liver, of all things?'
Through his head a whole drama passed,
about the value of fire and
the incomparable dignity of Titanic revolt.
A play coherent enough, and not bad artistically,
that he wanted to roar at Zeus with contempt.
But what he came out with was only:
'Why the liver, of all things?'

The vulture on his right is insatiable.
It knows its hangman's job, and does it openly.
Its beak, an excavator,
digs in, so that the mountains
quite onomatopoeically echo:
'That's why! That's why!'

This is and is not an answer
to the question that eats the hero
who, remote and forgotten by the world
in the stony deserts of the Caucasus,
still asserts his right to object,
so that the vast empty spaces
have grown hoarse with echoing:
'Why the liver, of all things?'

Pythia

Pythia crouches in antiquity
and foretells the future for us.

Whoever wants to see her
wastes a great deal of time
waiting, the queue is endless,
for the future is always in demand.

Yet I heard
what she prophesied
to all those ahead of me.

Tomorrow—she says –
or another day
something ordinary
or something extraordinary
will happen to you.

Alchemy

You ninety-nine elements,
come together, mingle, select yourselves
and give me happiness.

You ninety-nine elements,
I give you half my forehead:
arrange yourselves in the right proportions –
so much iron, so much gold, so much mercury –
and give me happiness.

You ninety-nine elements,
what shall I do with this disappointment,
with the star-shaped woman, with youth,
with the other ideals?
Give me happiness.

You ninety-nine elements
entered in the chart of my being,
look, into your alembic I throw yet another day,
another year,
another age . . .

To the Sea

I go again to the sea and converse with Ovid
whose verses like the Romanian coast roll along
so wide and subdued: waves that wait for the ice to break.

My poet, you that make what I sing two thousand years old,
ancient boundary stone on the edge of the Romanian language,
you the gulls have elected on to the governing board of our
epics,
of our song-grief you turned into Latin and gave
to the wind to carry to Rome and there, chiselled
into the column, await the Dacian prisoners.
You the first whom nostalgia, our *dor*, ate up
in those fields where the dust is sweet. You the first
to put your trust like a child in poetry's spellbinding power
and in help from abroad.
Sooner the Emperor would have sent experts to you at Tomi,
to change the climate, than see you back home,
your airy fame back in the purple of his retainers.
Who, he had said himself, could be better suited
to stand on the shore of the Pontus Euxinus, observing
how gradually it becomes the Black Sea, than a poet,
a good one, and one of repute—whom shall we send then,
whom?
And the choice fell on you, Ovid.
You were the first to occur to him because you
had just begun to be known, appreciated and talked about
like a bitter-sweet herb—that was your predicament.
Augustus liked your elegies, but only from a distance,
where they had the remedial effect the physicians prescribed,
an agreeable melancholy, after meals especially, when they
repeated on him...
The elegies were a medicine prescribed by the physicians
to save the Empire.
He even said: 'Why hasn't that boy sent us anything lately?
Force him to work, pinch him a bit, so that he'll grow
sad and Pontic, this wind is troubling me again, I'm gulping air...'
'People are asking why you had to relegate him,' a senator
timidly interjected.

'Suggest to them that he subverted the Empire,' the Emperor
                                        cynically smiled.
'Morally or materially?'—the exalted servant seemed hard
                                        of hearing.
'What, are you trying to drive me into a quandary? Both, let's
                                        say, a bit of each.
Ovid has done immense material *and* moral harm
to Latinity, and the citizens are indignant.
Or perhaps,' he considered, 'moral would be better,
after all we are an Imperium and don't stint the expenses
of a poet, but in moral matters we're strict: so, he corrupted
                                        our youth.'

Next day Augustus had second thoughts:
'No, for the time being no explanations, for anyone,
till we've thought of something more plausible'; and, to
                                        change the subject,
'What's Horace doing?' 'It's taken hold of him too, he's writing
no more odes but only *epodes*, nothing but epodes, an obscure
                                        sort of gibberish,
what shall we do about Horace, will he too become a case?'
'Let him be, let him be. Let's wait and see how he develops,
                                        he may have talent.
Maecenas and his house, after all, will take care of the cost
and we shall send him the bill with a troop of a hundred men.
But as for Ovid, he shall stay for a while yet
at Tomi, and no one shall hurt a hair of his head. We shall
think it over, meditate,' consult the augurs too.
No precipitous measures, where poets are concerned.'

Two thousand years have passed, and the Emperor
has not hit on appropriate action, he's thinking still.
But you must not give up hope, Ovid, you will be pardoned.
The matter was only provisional, an emergency, so be patient,
the problem will be resolved, as I said, when circumstances
                                        permit.

I go again to the sea and converse with Ovid,
the poet whose lines of fortune and arteries my earth senses
when he raises the Dobruja's broad hand to his brow.

Inebriation

The sea rolls pebbles in its mouth, copying Cicero
who, because he stammered, fed his affliction with pebbles
he picked up on the shore;
the age was so confused that words turned somersaults
and he had to tame them.

Or was it Demosthenes?
Whichever it was, one of them roared and ranted against
                                        injustice.
Nor does it make much difference: both were mighty orators.
What tirades they hurled at the sea!

Especially the one who thought that Carthage should be razed,
I believe it was Demosthenes, the one who later
had his head chopped off by the soldiers of Octavian Augustus,
                                        oh yes,
and his right arm, too, with which he gesticulated, while they
                                        said:
'No long speeches now, it's time to act'—and then went on
to raze Carthage, as he had predicted, as he had urged.
Or perhaps it was... Marcus Porcius Cato?
Confound it, there were so many of them, and all
had something sublime about them and believed in the word;
in other words: the proof of the pudding is in the eating.
Quod erat demonstrandum.
A pity, though, that they all came to a sticky end.
The strongest impression, however, that man made on me
who held his head under the axe: in his Philippics
the same holy anger simmers as in the bloody stump
after that absurd stroke. Damn it, what was his name?—I know
                he impressed me deeply, very deeply indeed.

Forget that I'm a daydreamer:
as usual, truth lies in the middle.
You are the world's middle, you are the truth, that's why I'm
                                        excited and stammer,
come, I'll whisper it into your ear.

It's Going to Rain

It's going to rain,
says God to himself, yawning
as he looks at the sky in which
not the tiniest cloud is visible.
These forty days, forty nights
my rheumatism has been playing me up.
Yes, there's a downpour coming.

Noah, hey there, Noah,
come to the fence,
there's something I want to tell you.

Asking Too Much?

'Suppose that, to give a few lectures,
daily you had to commute
between Heaven and Hell:
what would you take with you?'

'A book, a bottle of wine and a woman, Lord.
Is that asking too much?'

'Too much. We'll cross out the woman,
she would involve you in conversations,
put ideas into your head,
and your preparation would suffer.'

'I beseech you, cross out the book,
I'll write it myself, Lord, if only
I have the bottle of wine and the woman.
That's my wish and my need. Is it too much?'

'You're asking too much.
What, supposing that daily,
to give a few lectures, you had
to commute between Heaven and Hell, would
you take with you?'

'A bottle of wine and a woman,
if I may make so free.'
'That's what you wanted before, don't be obstinate,
it's too much, as you know. We'll cross out the woman.'

'What do you have against her, why do you persecute her?
Cross out the bottle rather,
wine weakens me, almost leaves me unable
to draw from my loved one's eyes
inspiration for those lectures.'

Silence, for minutes
or an eternity.
Respite. In which to forget.

'Well, suppose that to give
a few lectures you had to commute
daily between Heaven and Hell:
what would you take with you?'

'A woman, Lord, if I may make so free.'
'You're asking too much, we'll cross out the woman.'
'In that case cross out the lectures rather,
cross out Hell and Heaven for me,
it's either all or nothing.
Useless and vain my commuting would be between Heaven
and Hell.

How could I even begin to frighten and awe
those poor creatures in Hell –
without my teaching aid, the woman?
How strengthen the faith of the righteous in Heaven –
without the book's exegesis?
How endure all the differences
in temperature, light and pressure
between Heaven and Hell
if I have no wine
on the way
to give me a bit of courage?'

Sleep

My thoughts newly raked and
untrodden like a beach
after the onset of night.

In dreams her breasts look
like a capital S,
denoting a plural
in the language of things.

Chasm

Sometimes, gliding, I fall,
sometimes I rush through the ice
into the cosmic ocean.

There all sounds different.
I yearn for the opening,
the needle's ear, for my hoop.

Getting Matches

We're going out to get matches,
the firs say every morning
when they leave for the mountains
and the wind blows ideas
around their foreheads and

a cloud-mass rises, magma
conglomerations for future planets . . .
Only the resin that weeps from
their trunks knows
that their great migration,
their craving to burn,
has been mourned by us for a long time,
by us who stand
at the chasm's edge,

you at one end of the table,
I at the other.

AUTHORS PUBLISHED BY

BLOODAXE BOOKS

FLEUR ADCOCK	VICTORIA FORDE	JOHN MONTAGUE
GÖSTA ÅGREN	TUA FORSSTRÖM	EUGENIO MONTALE
ANNA AKHMATOVA	JIMMY FORSYTH	DAVID MORLEY
GILLIAN ALLNUTT	LINDA FRANCE	RICHARD MURPHY
SIMON ARMITAGE	ELIZABETH GARRETT	HENRY NORMAL
NEIL ASTLEY	ARTHUR GIBSON	SEAN O'BRIEN
ATTILA THE STOCKBROKER	PAMELA GILLILAN	JULIE O'CALLAGHAN
ANNEMARIE AUSTIN	ANDREW GREIG	JOHN OLDHAM
SHIRLEY BAKER	CHRIS GREENHALGH	OTTÓ ORBÁN
MARTIN BELL	JOHN GREENING	MICHEAL O'SIADHAIL
CONNIE BENSLEY	PHILIP GROSS	RUTH PADEL
STEPHEN BERG	JOSEF HANZLÍK	TOM PAULIN
ATTILIO BERTOLUCCI	TONY HARRISON	GYÖRGY PETRI
YVES BONNEFOY	GEOFF HATTERSLEY	TOM PICKARD
KARIN BOYE	ANNE HÉBERT	JILL PIRRIE
KAMAU BRATHWAITE	W.N. HERBERT	SIMON RAE
BASIL BUNTING	HAROLD HESLOP	DEBORAH RANDALL
CIARAN CARSON	DOROTHY HEWETT	IRINA RATUSHINSKAYA
JOHN CASSIDY	SELIMA HILL	MARIA RAZUMOVSKY
AIMÉ CÉSAIRE	FRIEDRICH HÖLDERLIN	PETER REDGROVE
SID CHAPLIN	MIROSLAV HOLUB	ANNE ROUSE
RENÉ CHAR	FRANCES HOROVITZ	CAROL RUMENS
GEORGE CHARLTON	DOUGLAS HOUSTON	LAWRENCE SAIL
EILÉAN NÍ CHUILLEANÁIN	JOHN HUGHES	EVA SALZMAN
KILLARNEY CLARY	PAUL HYLAND	PETER SANSOM
BRENDAN CLEARY	STEPHEN KNIGHT	SAPPHO
JACK CLEMO	PHILIPPE JACCOTTET	DAVID SCOTT
HARRY CLIFTON	KATHLEEN JAMIE	JO SHAPCOTT
JACK COMMON	VLADIMÍR JANOVIC	SIR ROY SHAW
STEWART CONN	B.S. JOHNSON	ELENA SHVARTS
NOEL CONNOR	LINTON KWESI JOHNSON	MATT SIMPSON
DAVID CONSTANTINE	JOOLZ	LEMN SISSAY
CHARLOTTE CORY	JENNY JOSEPH	DAVE SMITH
JENI COUZYN	SYLVIA KANTARIS	KEN SMITH
HART CRANE	JACKIE KAY	SEAN MAYNE SMITH
ADAM CZERNIAWSKI	BRENDAN KENNELLY	STEPHEN SMITH
FRED D'AGUIAR	SIRKKA-LIISA KONTTINEN	EDITH SÖDERGRAN
PETER DIDSBURY	JEAN HANFF KORELITZ	PIOTR SOMMER
STEPHEN DOBYNS	DENISE LEVERTOV	MARIN SORESCU
MAURA DOOLEY	HERBERT LOMAS	LEOPOLD STAFF
KATIE DONOVAN	MARION LOMAX	PAULINE STAINER
JOHN DREW	EDNA LONGLEY	EIRA STENBERG
IAN DUHIG	FEDERICO GARCÍA LORCA	MARTIN STOKES
HELEN DUNMORE	GEORGE MacBETH	RABINDRANATH TAGORE
STEPHEN DUNSTAN	PETER McDONALD	JEAN TARDIEU
JACQUES DUPIN	DAVID McDUFF	D.M. THOMAS
G.F. DUTTON	MEDBH McGUCKIAN	R.S. THOMAS
LAURIS EDMOND	MAIRI MacINNES	TOMAS TRANSTRÖMER
ALISTAIR ELLIOT	CHRISTINE McNEILL	MARINA TSVETAYEVA
STEVE ELLIS	OSIP MANDELSTAM	MIRJAM TUOMINEN
ODYSSEUS ELYTIS	GERALD MANGAN	FRED VOSS
EURIPIDES	E.A. MARKHAM	NIGEL WELLS
DAVID FERRY	WILLIAM MARTIN	C.K. WILLIAMS
EVA FIGES	GLYN MAXWELL	JOHN HARTLEY WILLIAMS
SYLVA FISCHEROVÁ	HENRI MICHAUX	JAMES WRIGHT
TONY FLYNN	ADRIAN MITCHELL	BENJAMIN ZEPHANIAH

For a complete catalogue of books published by Bloodaxe, pleaee write to:

Bloodaxe Books Ltd, P.O. Box 1SN, Newcastle upon Tyne NE99 1SN.